Foss Is the Boss

By Carmel Reilly

It is hot.

Foss the cat sits in the sun.

Foss looks up.

Russ the dog runs in.

He did not see Foss yet.

Russ looks at the tin.

Foss gets up.

Russ looks at Foss.

Russ looks at the tin.

Russ is big.

Foss is not as big as Russ.

But Foss is **very** cross!

Foss will not let Russ
get her tin.

Foss hops on to the sill.

She puffs up.

Russ looks up at Foss.

Foss is big and gruff!

Foss will not let Russ get to the tin.

Russ runs off in a huff.

It's a loss for Russ.

But a win for Foss.

Foss **is** the boss!

CHECKING FOR MEANING

1. What was Foss doing at the start of the story? *(Literal)*

2. What does Russ want? *(Literal)*

3. Do you think Russ will come back again? Why? *(Inferential)*

EXTENDING VOCABULARY

hiss	Revise the words in the story that are examples of onomatopoeia, i.e. *hiss, ruff, yip*. Remind students that these words imitate the sound made by the character or object in the text.
sill	What is the *sill*? Where is it? Why does Foss get up on the sill?
gruff	What is the meaning of *gruff*? What other words have a similar meaning? E.g. grumpy, angry, stern. When have you been gruff?

MOVING BEYOND THE TEXT

1. What do pet cats usually eat?

2. Is cat food suitable for a dog to eat? Why?

3. What should the owner of Foss do to stop Russ coming into the yard again?

4. Do all pets get along well together? Why?

SPEED SOUNDS

| ff | ll | ss | zz |

PRACTICE WORDS

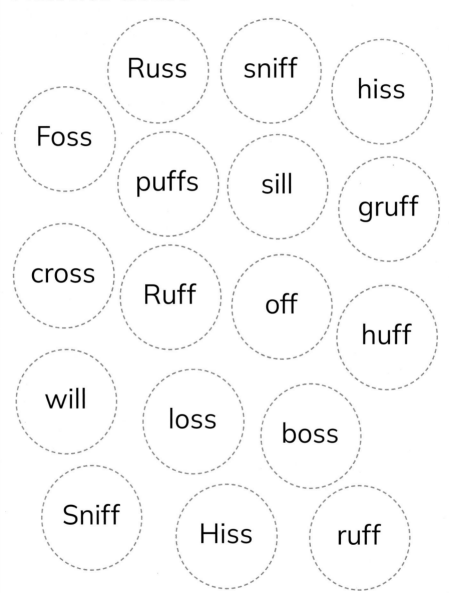

Russ

sniff

hiss

Foss

puffs

sill

gruff

cross

Ruff

off

huff

will

loss

boss

Sniff

Hiss

ruff